The Last Revolution

Play

Solomon C. A. Awuzie

Mwanaka Media and Publishing Pvt Ltd,
Chitungwiza Zimbabwe
*
Creativity, Wisdom and Beauty

Publisher: *Mmap*
Mwanaka Media and Publishing Pvt Ltd
24 Svosve Road, Zengeza 1
Chitungwiza Zimbabwe
mwanaka@yahoo.com
mwanaka13@gmail.com
www.africanbookscollective.com/publishers/mwanaka-media-and-publishing
https://facebook.com/MwanakaMediaAndPublishing/

Distributed in and outside N. America by African Books Collective
orders@africanbookscollective.com
www.africanbookscollective.com

ISBN: 978-1-77928-529-4
EAN: 9781779285294

© Solomon C. A Awuzie 2025

All rights reserved.
No part of this book may be reproduced or transmitted in any form or by any means, mechanical or electronic, including photocopying and recording, or be stored in any information storage or retrieval system, without written permission from the publisher

DISCLAIMER
All views expressed in this publication are those of the author and do not necessarily reflect the views of *Mmap*.

…Anthony Awuzie, Anna Awuzie,

Isidore Diala:

All these are revolutionaries. Those whose Vigil fire swayed

and forged a raw dream into gold.

Also dedicated to:

Kin Saro-Wiwa, Ezenwa-Ohieto

and all others

to whom dreams danced

only to fall to

stillborn.

Author's Word

It was in 2004 that I first thought of what gave birth to the first Nigerian coup. And after discussing the coup with my friend, Chukwuma Ibezute, I decided to do an adaptation of it in 2005 for my first degree project at the Imo State University, Owerri. But not until in 2009 at University of Ibadan that I met a group of friends who stirred the old horrible feeling into my mind, with their mind pricking discussions.

Having encountered tribalism in all the places I travelled and seeing unpatriotism glaring in every face and every action of our people; having experienced the government's carelessness to the welfare of the people and the people's nonchalance over the existence of the government; I contemplated the relationship between all that had happened before the coup with what is happening now in our country. At such I decided to adapt the first Nigerian coup in such a way that all that led to the coup could be pin pointed.

The last revolution caused us so much pains and trouble; it even planted disunity among us. But even in the face of these facts, I will like to make it known that we cannot amend our today or dream of a fulfilled tomorrow without looking back to the past—not to condemn or praise anybody but that we might learn from the past.

Solomon C.A. Awuzie

... Patriotism, fellows, implies action not words!

Ola Rotimi (Who is a Patriot?)

Dramatic Personae

Major Nzeogwu
Major Ademoyega
Major Ifeanjuna
Major Okafor — the revolutionaries
Major Gbulie
Major Onwuatuegwu
Captain Anuforo
Captain Ude

Captain Udeaja
Uche Chukwumerije
Major-General Ironsi
Lieutenant-Colonel Gowon
Major Madiebo — enemies of the revolution
Lieutenant-Colonel Nwawo
Tafawa Balewa
Coloniel K Mohammed
Lieutenant-Colonel Unegbu
The Sardauna

Captains
Subalterns
Soldiers
Politicians

Act One

I

Enter Cadets, matching onto the stage followed by Sergeants and an RSM. Cadets lining up in platoons of seven. Enter the Sardauna, three Ministers and a Colonel.

Colonel:

Gentlemen Cadets, the premier of the North, the Sardauna of Sokoto and these honourable Ministers are here for official visit and inspection. (*pauses*) (*Colonel calls the RSM and orders him to carry on with the ceremony. RSM salutes and orders the Sergeants. One of the Sergeants commands the Cadets:* "remove head dress!" *They all remove their caps and raise them up. After a while, he commands that they replace it and they comply.*) You can address them now, sir.

Sardauna:

(*silent for a while*) Let me go round first. (*The Colonel leads the Sardauna amidst the platoons of Cadets. After the inspection, the Sardauna returns to the podium. He takes a deep breath and catches a glimpse of one of the Cadets in the front roll and quickly calls his attention.*) You, where do you come from? (*There is silence.*) I am talking to you!

Cadet:

Me? (*Sardauna nods*) I come from Nigeria, sir!

Sardauna:

Yes, I know, but where exactly in Nigeria?

Cadet:

(*The Cadet hesitates but later speaks.*) I am from the north.

Gbulie:

(*aside*) How can this man begin his address by creating in us the feeling of disunity?

Sardauna:

(*nods and starts addressing them in Hausa.*) You all have started to look like real soldiers. I like that! That means the future of Nigerian Army is bright.

Nzeogwu:

(*to Gbulie*) Ben, don't worry yourself. We will teach that bloody politician a lesson he will never forget.

****

Federal house. Enter Politicians of different tribes.

Politician 1:

I…I was telling the minister to…to bring the money for…for the project for us to sh…share and he started telling me the…the old story about Nigeria. You know, I laughed at him and told him that…that this country is a marriage of different peo…people and different tribes and should be seen from that light—that the money is more useful when it is shared.

Politician 11:

When I hear people talk about united Nigeria, I become annoyed because to me they are saying rubbish. I wonder who told them that I care about the country. I am not a minister because of anybody, my comfort is my interest for now. Maybe when the country gets better I will see the need to think towards that light.

Politician 111:

I don't believe in this so called marriage. I am first an Ijaw man before I am a Nigerian. (*pauses*) Let's forget this Nigeria talk for now and concentrate on how to get that money and make sure the money is shared.

Politician 11:

So how do we go about it?

Politician 111:

Somebody should call him, let me talk to him.

Politician 1:

But I…I have already…alr…discussed it with him and he re…refused.

Politician 111:

Maybe you didn't discuss it well with him. Remember he is a politician. You have to make him see reasons why the money should be shared and you also tell him that he is to get a big share of the money.

Politician 11:

Okay, let me go and call him. (*Politician 11 leaves*)

Politician 1:

That man ne...needs to be talked to. I don't know why he is alw...always behaving like that. (*Enter Politician 11 with Politician IV*)

Politician IV:

You sent for me.

Politician 111:

Yes. You see, I called you here in respect to that money assigned to your office...

Politician IV:

That money is set aside for federal road project...

Politician 111:

Please release the money, let us share it. Be assured that you have our backup.

Politician IV:

(*hisses*) ...but...but!

Politician 11:

Since the money is coming from your office, you will have the highest share.

Politician IV:

(*gasps*) Like how many percent will be my share?

Politician III:

Forty percent for you and sixty percent for us. Or what do you think?

Politician IV:

Well, that is okay! (*pauses*) Okay, let me pay it into your accounts tomorrow. (*looks into their faces*)

All:

Okay! (*They keep discussing as they leave the stage.*)

****

Selection Board, Kaduna: an office with Nigerian and military flags. Cadets gather in anticipation of the unpublished list of those selected for the army. Enter Chukwumerije and Ademoyega from different directions.

Ademoyega:

The list is not yet published (*tries to ask a nearby Cadet. The Cadet turns away and walks towards another Cadet who is probably from his ethnic group.*)

Chukwumerije:

(*turns, sees Ademoyega and then walks towards him.*) I guess you also came for the list?

Ademoyega:

Yes! (*pauses*) Do you know whether the list will still be published today?

Chukwumerije:

I think so; since it was announced it would be published today. (*Cadets are seen walking up and down the stage.*)

Ademoyega:

I hope to find my name on the list.

Chukwumerije:

(*smiles.*) I know you are a southerner as I am and maybe you have not heard that the board will make their selection by quota system. (*A group of Cadets are seen conversing at a corner of the stage though in mime.*)

Ademoyega:

Really? (*There is an echo of laughter from behind. They turn to see those laughing and then turn to each other again.*)

Chukwumerije:

And the Northerners have already been billed to be fifty percent.

Ademoyega:

But the number of Cadets from the South is more than those from the North!

Chukwumerije:

That is the problem! (*Enter Ifeajuna from the office, dressed in a Lieutenant uniform.*) That Lieutenant looks familiar. Let's ask him. (*They walk towards him.*) Excuse sir! (*Lieutenant Ifeajuna sees them and stops.*)

Ifeajuna:

Yes, who are you? (*steals a glance at the office and returns his attention to them.*)

Ademoyega:

I am Adewale Ademoyega and this is my friend.

Chukwumerije:

My name is Uche Chukwumerije.

Ifeajuna:

How can I help you?

Ademoyega:

We are among those who applied to be selected into the Army and from the news reaching us, the board will do their selection by quota system.

Ifeajuna:

Yes?

Ademoyega:

What's our fate sir; I mean those from the South?

Ifeajuna:

I don't know! (*pauses.*) Just pray your names are among those selected. (*forces out a smile.*)

Chukwumerije:

But why the quota system?

Ifeajuna:

It is a long story but one thing you should know is that the British has agreed with the Balewa government to handover an Army, which will be more than fifty percent Northern.

Ademoyega:

(*nods his head.*) Is this also the reason the British government has been delaying the Nigerianisation of the officers corps and the Nigerian Army?

Ifeajuna:

Yes! (*pauses.*) Their aim is to set tribal confusion rolling while they have the time to tele-guide our political and economic development. (*Enter Okwechime, dressed in a Captain uniform.*) But there is hope. Don't worry I will introduce you to Captain Kaduna Nzeogwu.

Okwechime:

Lieutenant Ifeajuna, you are here?

Chukwumerije & Ademoyega:

Mourn sir!

Okwechime:

Mourn!

Ifeajuna:

(*turns to Captain Okwechime.*) Captain, I am telling these boys what they should know. (*pauses.*) Young men, all these things I have so far pointed out to you can still be put in order.

Ademoyega:

How sir?

Ifeajuna:

(*smiles.*) Don't worry just come into the Army. I believe so much that it is the Army that can save this country. (*pauses.*) I think I should be on my way now.

Ademoyega & Chukwumerije:

Thank you sir! (*Lieutenant Ifeajuna leaves the stage.*)

Okwechime:

The Army needs young men like you. (*Enter an officer with a list. There is a stampede. He posts the list on the wall and walks back into the office.*) You can go and check your names now. (*They leave Captain Okwechime in check of their names. They return wearing happy faces.*) Did you see your names?

Ademoyega:

Yes!

Okwechime:

Congratulations! (*shakes hands with them.*) You are welcome into the Army.

Ademoyega & Chukwumerije:

Thank you sir! (*Captain Okwechime leaves the stage.*)

Chukwumerije:

(*turns to Ademoyega.*) I told you, that Lieutenant looks familiar!

Ademoyega:

Yes, you mean Lieutenant Ifeajuna.

Chukwumerije:

Ifeajuna! Oh yes! So he is now in the Army?

Ademoyega:

Is he related to you?

Chukwumerije:

I still doubt he is the person we saw in that Army uniform.

Ademoyega:

What'd he do?

Chukwumerije:

When I was in the college, stories were told about those who deserted their groups at the time of action and Ifeajuna was among them. And now he is in the Army.

Ademoyega:

Uche, that was only in the college. He's now in the Army and if such behaviour shows up, it'll be taken care of.

Chukwumerije:

Well, let's hope so. (*pauses*.)

Ademoyega:

Uche, Lieutenant Ifeajuna said something about one Captain Kaduna Nzeogwu. What do you think that statement is for?

Chukwumerije:

I don't know (*pauses*). I think it is connected to the issue of the quota system.

Ademoyega:

I think it's more than that (*pauses*). Do you know the Captain?

Chukwumerije:

You mean Captain Nzeogwu?

Ademoyega:

Yes!

Chukwumerije:

Yes, I have heard about him. But I have not really seen him. (*pauses*) They said he is a very good man, a very good soldier and a patriot.

Ademoyega:

Okay! *(He gasps)* let's go! (*They walk out of stage.*)

(Snooze)

II

Single Officer's room. Enter Ademoyega and Ifeajuna. Ademoyega is dressed in a short trouser and a T-shirt and is holding a newspaper while Ifeajuna is dressed in a Major uniform. Ademoyega ushers Ifeajuna into a nearby seat.

Ifeajuna:

Why are we not going to blame the Balewa government? Is it also true that the British government taught them to be corrupt? I think the answer is no. (*pauses*) Yes, I've almost forgot to ask you about your friend.

Ademoyega:

Which of my friends?

Ifeajuna:

The one with whom you came to the selection board then.

Ademoyega:

Oh, Uche Chukwumerije!

Ifeajuna:

What about him?

Ademoyega:

He didn't continue after the selection.

Ifeajuna:

Why?

Ademoyega:

It's a long story. (*pauses*) It was immediately after the selection that he changed his mind. He didn't turn up to be enlisted into the Army and his place remained vacant both in the plane from Kano to London and even at the Mons Officer Cadet School where we were to be trained for six months.

Ifeajuna:

(*clears his throat*) Why? This is strange.

Ademoyega:

I later found out what was wrong when I met him some months later on the street of Lagos. I was… (*The stage becomes dim all of a sudden and beside it comes a faint light which later blazes the lower side of the stage. Enter Ademoyega, dressed in a Lieutenant uniform and enter Chukwumerije. Lieutenant Ademoyega sees him (loud shouts.)* Uche! Is this you? (*Chukwumerije is shocked.*)

Chukwumerije:

Wale! (*They embrace each other.*) It is nice seeing you again. How is life treating you?

Ademoyega:

Very well but… (*pauses.*) Yes! Uche, why didn't you turn up?

Chukwumerije:

Oh! The Army? (*Lieutenant Ademoyega nods.*) The problem was that after our names were published, I met one of the white professors who taught me then in Ibadan. I told him that I have gone to join the Army for revolutionary reasons. But do you know, he warned me that the Army is the most conservative and least revolutionary of all national institutions. I thought over what he said and found out that it is true and then decided to find a more revolutionary movement outside the Army.

Ademoyega:

(*shakes his head*) No! Uche, no! That's only from British point of view.

Chukwumerije:

But I've decided to leave the Army.

Ademoyega:

No! N… (*Light fades out and all of a sudden light returns on the main stage again. And we see Ademoyega still discussing with Ifeajuna…*) I assured my friend course, but Uche had already agreed with the professor and it was pointless whipping a dead horse.

Ifeajuna:

And who said that the Army can't be revolutionary?

Ademoyega:

My pain is that Uche refused to look into history so as to know that the Army can be revolutionary. At least he should have considered revolutionary Armies like the Genghis Khan's Army of the Thirteenth Century, the Cromwellian Army of the Seventeenth Century, the Napoleonic Army of the early Nineteenth Century, the revolutionary Bolshevik Army of Russia and the Army of Chairman Mao Tse Tung of China in the Mid-twentieth Century… (*There is a knock*) Please, come in! (*Enter Anuforo in a captain uniform. He salutes and Ademoyega gives him a seat to sit down.*)

Anuforo:

I was driving to NMTC. When I got to this place, I deemed it important stopping by to greet you.

Ademoyega:

You've done well. (*turns to Major Ifeajuna.*) Major Ifeajuna, this is Captain Christian Anuforo.

Ifeajuna:

Captain, you are welcome!

Anuforo:

Thank you, sir!

Ademoyega:

He also joined the Army for revolutionary reason.

Ifeajuna:

(*nods*) That's good! (*stands up and shakes hands with him.*) You are welcome once again.

Anuforo:

Thank you, sir!

Ademoyega:

Captain Anuforo, this is Major Emmanuel Ifeajuna whom I told you about the last time we met.

Anuforo:

(*salutes again.*) Ifeajuna, the six feet, eight inches jump gold medalist?

Ifeajuna:

Exactly! (*They laugh.*)

Anuforo:

Major, I've heard so much about you.

Ifeajuna:

Really?

Anuforo:

Most importantly, all you have been doing to see that there is a turn of event in this corrupt country of ours.

Ademoyega:

That was what we were discussing before you came in.

Anuforo:

You talk as if it is only you who talk about it. The discussion is all over the street. Whenever you see two Nigerians discussing, the theme of their discussion is nothing but this corruption that has eaten deep into this country.

Ifeajuna:

And tribalism-the most dreadful of our country's insuperable monster.

Anuforo:

And that one my brother-Nigerian's number one killer disease, a tanker-worm as old as the hills - a fundamental factor of the problems of Nigerian unity.

Ademoyega:

The politicians and the public officers have indeed let the nation down. What they do in office is just to enrich themselves with the ten percent takings and kickbacks from contractors. Even as if that was not enough, embezzlement is on the increase.

Anuforo:

Like yesterday, it was reported that there was physical combat in the parliament as usual between one tribe and another.

Ifeajuna:

That is what I was telling Ademoyega before you came in. The Federal parliament is now an inter-tribal battle field.

Ademoyega:

And you say this country will be better under those tribalists who parade themselves as politicians.

Anuforo:

Comrades… (*pauses*) I think I should be on my way now. This topic you have chosen this evening is never ending.

Ademoyega:

Yes! Lest I forget, if you get there, please tell Major Nzeogwu that Major Ifeajuna has been posted to the South but now as the Brigade Major of the second Brigade based in Apapa.

Anuforo:

Okay sir! (*turns to Major Ifeajuna.*) Congratulation sir!

Ifeajuna:

Thank you. (*Captain Anuforo turns to leave and Ademoyega calls his attention.*)

(Snooze)

III

Politicians gather while their supporters are seated at the corner of the stage. There is noise at the background—people are protesting.

Politician 1:

Everybody settle down! Please settle down, let us begin the day's business. (*The noise continues. Politician 1 beckons on the chief whip who has been standing at another corner of the stage and he comes forward*) Please tell those people over there to be quiet. (*The chief whip walks over to the supporters.*)

Chief whip:

Please, be quiet let's start the day's business. Please be quiet.

Politician 1:

(*continues*) I wish to begin by thanking the 'House' for making sure there is a turn of events in this region. None of us has been happy ever since it was discovered that our former Premier, Chief Akintola has been doing everything under his power to give away the in-house plans of our regional house and the national party to the NPC and the Sardauna his friend. Even by replacing him with Chief Adegbenro I think things will work very well and with the required secrecy. (*The people start making noise and it becomes almost uncontrollable. The Chief Whip tries to calm the people to no avail. The speaker, Prince Adedoyin intervenes by hitting the gavel. The noise continues. All of a sudden, the supporters rise and began to dance towards the middle stage.*)

Chief Whip:

What is all this for? Stop! (*The people ignore him and continue dancing. He tries to intervene by forcing some people back to their seats. He is pushed away; he falls while the people continue dancing. Prince Adedoyin, the speaker, picks up the gavel again and hits it. One of the dancers quickly ceases the mace on the table and aims it at the speaker. The speaker dodges it and it smashes beside him. Enter the federal police. The people disperse. The police arrest the rioters and lead them out of stage.*)

Prince Adedoyin:

The mace has been broken so we cannot continue with our deliberation today again (*pauses, turns to the Chief Whip.*) But who are they?

Chief Whip:

They are the supporters of Chief Akintola and his new political party.

Prince Adedoyin:

You mean the NNDP?

Chief Whip:

Today's deliberation is closed till further notice. (*They file out of the stage.*)

****

NNDP Secretariat. Enter politicians with their supporters.

Politician 1:

Our man has done it! We told them that we own the West. (*Enter Chief Akintola. The people cheer him. He raises his hands and waves at them.*) The federal government has declared a state of emergency on this region because of our Chief (*The people cheer again*) and has appointed Dr. Majekodunmi, the federal minister of * Health, as the sole Administrator of the region. Hail Chief Akintola! Hail Chief Akintola! (*The people cheer, chanting his name and he raises his hands at them. Again, while the politician stops them again.*) The federal government will be sending the Third Battalion of the Nigerian Army down to Ibadan. I advise all of you to be quiet and go about your businesses because the whole situation is under control.

Chief Akintola:

(*raising his hand*) NNDP!

People:

Power!

Chief Akintola:

NNDP!

People:

Power!

Chief Akintola:

I say NNDP!

People:

We say power!

Chief Akintola:

I want to let you know that we are in control of this region. (*people cheer and he waves at them to settle down*) You all know that there will be a new vote in a few months time. I want you all to come out and vote but that does not mean that your vote will really count. Even if nobody votes that day, I am still going to win that election. (*People cheer*) NNDP!

People:

Power!

Chief Akintola:

Power!

People:

NNDP! (*People start chanting Chief Akintola's name. Drummers join and the people start dancing and danced off stage.*)

(Snooze)

IV

Enter Major Ifeajuna, Major Ademoyega and Major Chudesokei in civilian attires.

Ifeajuna:

Please, sit down while we wait for the rest.

Chuke-sokei:

We still have about twenty minutes to the time. They will soon arrive. (*Enter Captain Anuforo and Major Okafor.*)

Ifeajuna:

You are welcome!

Anuforo & Okafor:

Thank you. (*They sit down. Enter Major Chukwuka.*)

Anuforo:

Major Chukwuka, it seems you have been walking behind us.

Chukwuka:

So you just came? (*Major Anuforo nods. Enter Nzeogwu. They all settled down.*)

Nzeogwu:

This meeting is going to be very brief. So let us begin with the national Anthem. (*They stand up and sing the national Anthem.*) From the way things are moving in this country, if there is no intervention the country will find itself in a situation where breaking up will be the only way forward. It is on this ground that we have gathered here today; to plan how this country could be saved from its imminent doom. (*pauses and signals Major Ifeajuna.*)

Ifeajuna:

(*clears his throat*) I believe all of us who have been invited here joined the Army for revolutionary reason and this is the time to put our heads together and come out with how to go about our dreams. (*pauses and signals back to Major Nzeogwu.*)

Nzeogwu:

(*continues.*) Another reason why we have gathered here is to pry into the plan which Major Ifeajuna, Major Ademoyega and I had set out for this mission. Its aim is to ask for suggestions and make possible amendments in order to strengthen the revolutionary dream. So let me call on Major Ademoyega to read out the plan to everybody's hearing. (Major Ademoyega brings out a wrapped paper and reads.)

Ademoyega:

Major Ifeajuna, Major Nzeogwu and I had suggested the following: (*reading now*) First it is going to be a nationwide coup. Secondly, the coup will happen in a day. Thirdly, the coup will start simultaneously in all the regions of the Federation. (*Major Ademoyega pauses. Major Chude-Sokei and Major Chukwuka nod their heads, delightfully.*) We also agreed that the targets of the revolution would be the political leaders and all their military collaborators because it is only through their removal from office that the problem of this country can be solved.

Chude-Sokei:

(cuts in.) Are the targeted personalities going to be killed or arrested?

Anuforo:

I think they should be killed.

Chukwuka:

No! Killing them all will make the people see us as officers in desperate need of power rather than revolutionaries. I suggest they should be arrested.

Chude-Sokei:

I support what Major Chukwuka said.

Nzeogwu:

Okay, it is taken. They should be arrested but in case there is resistance of any kind, they should be killed.

Ademoyega:

(reads again.) Our target political leaders should include the President, Prime minister, the four regional premiers and the minister of finance. This people are: one, the Right Honourable Doctor Nnamdi Azikiwe, the president of the Federal Republic and Commander-in-Chief of the Nigerian Armed forces. A valerian politician who has been in the forefront of the titanic struggle for independence. He remains a nationalist leader and the father figure of Nigerian unity but has in recent time been found with traits of tribalism *(pauses)*. The second person: Alhaji Sir Abubakar Tafawa Balewa, a leader who

has risen to the top on a tribal ticket, an agent of tribalism and ally of the Western capitalist interest. He is the head of a puppet government and rules as though he has no mind of his own (*pauses*). The third is Doctor Michael Okpara, the premier of the Eastern Region. He is a pragmatic politician but though dynamic. He is corrupt. He is widely seen to believe that the traditional method of seeking political solutions through compromise is no longer adequate (*pauses*). Alhaji Sir Ahmadu Bello, the premier of the Northern Region and the Sardauna of Sokoto. He wields monumental power. He is an arch – tribalist and therefore an implacable enemy of the Nigerian unity. He is said to be directing the affairs of Federation from Kaduna (*pauses*). Chief Samuel Ladoke Akintola, the thin-voiced premier of the Western Region. He was ascribed to have rigged the last Western general elections, and hence the outbreak of horrendous violence in that region. He is known for mean political intrigues, and was seen to be running from pillar to post in the Nigerian political arena. His name, moreover, is connected with the secret nocturnal meetings being held at Kaduna at the Northern Regional Premier's residence. He would go to any length to seek the destruction of his political opponents (*pauses*). Chief Festus Okotie- Eboh, the federal finance minister who is involved in a shady shoe business deal. Though he had made a career of flaunting his wealth, he is seen as a man of dubious means (pauses). While among their military collaborators, only the top echelon and those holding strategic positions are to be targeted.

Okafor:

Please, why not be specific as you did with the politicians, so that we can know.

Ifeajuna:

Why not be patient? I feel he is coming to that.

Ademoyega:

(*pauses*) Those officers should include: Major General Aguyi Ironsi, the GOC of the Nigerian Army; the Commanders of Nigerian two Brigades, Brigadier Ademulegun and Brigadier Maimalari; the Chief of staff of the Army Headquarter, Colonel Kur Mohammed; the Adjutant General of the Army, Lieutenant Colonel Pam; the Deputy Commander NDA, Colonel Shodeinde and the Quarter-Master-General of the Army, Lieutenant-Colonel Unegbu (*pauses*).

I will go on to mention these officers again and their profiles. First, Major-General Johnson Thompson Umunakwe Aguyi Ironsi is the general officer commanding the Nigerian Army. A hard-drinking, slow- speaking introvert who had risen to high ranks, and had been trained at Eaton Hall and Camberley Staff College. He is both inept and inefficient - hardly the calibre of officer to command an army (*pauses*). Secondly, Brigadier Samuel Adesujo Ademulegun, the commander of first Brigade. A first-class soldier, immensely talented and versed in military strategy and tactics, he is however, every inch a tribalist, as well as overly ambitions and vindictive. He would bend over backwards to please any high-ranking politician if by doing so, he also serves a private end. A noted schemer, he is one of those whose names were associated with the secret nocturnal meetings being held at the premier's residence at Kaduna (*pauses*). Thirdly,

Brigadier Zakariya Maimalari, the commander of the second Brigade. A brilliant soldier, Sandhurst-trained and good-looking in the bargain. He is also a tribalist (*pauses*). Lieutenant Colonel Yakubu Pam, trained at Sandhurst and Camberley Staff College. He is the Adjutant-General at the Army Headquarter. Following the OP-Adam III, which he and Brigadier Ademulegun took-guided from Kaduna, it is clear that he is notorious. He was also said to have been instrumental in replacing Anuforo after the latter had refused to release some pro-NNA politicians caught with sizable caches of illegal arms and ammunition.

Anuforo:

Very true!

Ademoyega:

Besides, it was rumoured that his ultra-modern two-storey building at Kaduna is a gift from the NPC politicians who had gained from his friendship (*pauses*). Colonel C.A. Sodeinde is the enigmatic second in command of the first Brigade and the Deputy Commandant of the Nigerian Defence Academy. Dull, indolent and inefficient, he is widely regarded as redundant and is therefore given to brooding. He too is deeply steeped in tribalism. (There is silence. Major Ademoyega turns to Major Nzeogwu.) Please, if there is any name that is missed out, do well to inform the house.

Okafor:

What of the commander of the fourth Battalion which is based in Ibadan and which is the most politicized unit of the Army, Colonel Largema? (*Major Nzeogwu notes it and signals for more suggestions.*)

Anuforo:

I want to know if officers like Brigadier Ogundipe, Lieutenant-Colonel Gowon, Lieutenant-Colonel Fajuyi and other Colonel Njoku, Lieutenants Effiong, Ojukwu, Ejoor, Banjo and Bassey not going to constitute a threat to the revolution?

Nzeogwu:

I think the issue about officers who are not holding strategic positions has been bothering me also but I solemnly believe that if this revolution holds and gains ground those officers will not be in our way. (*signals Major Ademoyega to continue.*)

Ademoyega:

We agreed that the field of operation is to be divided into the North and South zones. The reason is to keep in line with the two-brigade structure of the Nigerian Army and to facilitate command so as to attain the desired goal. We have also decided to define the commands of each officers of this revolutionary council. And on this ground we suggested that while Major Nzeogwu should command the operation for the North, Major Chude-Sokei should command the operation for the east and mid-west. Major Ifeajuna and myself should command the operation for Lagos and the west respectively.

Nzeogwu:

Does any of you have any objection to this? (*There is silence*.) Okay!

Ademoyega:

(*continues*) And finally, the operation is to be carried out in three phases. Phase one is to deal with the necessary preliminaries which is to include preparation, planning and rehearsal. Phase two is to consist of the coup itself and mopping-up. The first thing to do as soon as it is zero hour is to move troops and armoured fighting vehicles to Jebba and Makurdi to hold the Benue and Niger bridges with a view of preventing the movement of any troops opposed to the revolution to and from the North. It is also under this phase that each zonal leader or his appointed representative will go on air with a crisply worded announcement. This must be done when the coup has gone under way, but not before contacting Major Nzeogwu, by telephone. The dawn broadcast is to alert fellow Nigerians as to the demise of the First Republic, announce the suspension of the constitution, describe all the political parties in the country, depose martial law until further notice, impose a dusk-to-dawn curfew and appeal for calm. And phase three is to be concerned with both the re-organisation and government. The arrangement for this phase is that, having successfully carried out the coup, each zonal leader is to dispatch immediately to Lagos, a team or teams of honest patriotic and reliable civilians who are to join Chief Obafemi Awolowo and a number of specially chosen military men in establishing an interim administration. A unitary system of government has been chosen as a workable system for this country. And the three regions of the country hitherto strongholds of tribalism are to be split up by an act of decree into small debilitated provinces so as not to jeopardize the future of the system (pauses and signals Major Nzeogwu).

Nzeogwu:

It is important to note that we need more officers who can turn out their commands for our use. So, on this note I urge all of you to work hard to get more officers to join us. With this I call this meeting over. (*They all stand up, sing the national Anthem and then depart.*)

(Snooze)

ACT TWO

I

Enter Major Nzeogwu, restless. Enter a soldier. He hands Nzeogwu a letter. Major Nzeogwu reads through it, tears it and signals the soldier to go. Enter Major Ademoyega.

Ademoyega:

You look unhappy. What's the matter?

Nzeogwu:

The lady whom I am to go on reconnaissance to the Sardauna's castle did not turn up, only for her to send me a letter saying rubbish.

Ademoyega:

Don't let that bother you. We can always get another lady for the purpose. (*Major Nzeogwu cheers up.*) So have you been able to get any more officers to our side?

Nzeogwu:

Wale, (*smiles*) it is not easy. Though I have not been able to get new officers to join us, I have succeeded in introducing what I call 'exercise Damisa' to the troops I command.

Ademoyega:

What does that mean?

Nzeogwu:

'Exercise Damisa' means training troop of officers with the aim of using the troops for the D-day, without the knowledge of the troop.

Ademoyega:

This is great. (*nods his head.*)

Nzeogwu:

I will like the same to be staged in the South (*pauses*). When you go back please tell Major Ifeajuna to make sure such exercise is organized in Lagos in a way similar to what I have done here.

Ademoyega:

It's important!

Nzeogwu:

And Wale, I hope you and Major Ifeajuna have started doing the reconnaissance of the various locations that you must take over on the D-day.

Ademoyega:

Yes! (*pauses.*) We've been doing our best. Before I forget, Major Ifeajuna said I should inform you that Major Chude-Sokei sent him a message that he is soon to travel to India for a course and that I should tell you to fix D-day today because, as you know, Major Chude-Sokei is our strong man for the East. If he leaves, there may be no other person to replace him.

Nzeogwu:

Wale see! We can only fix D-day when we are sure all the political leaders are in the country. Anything aside, we miss our target. (*Pauses.*) Please send a signal to Major Chude-Sokei to postpone his travel for at least two months.

Ademoyega:

But can't we work out the date when all the political leaders can be in the country today?

Nzeogwu:

We can, but that is only if you have all the information about their movements.

Ademoyega:

I think I have all the information

Nzeogwu:

Okay, what is the information like?

Ademoyega:

I've been informed that the Sardauna will lead the Umaru Hadi group out of the country soon and that they are to return to Kaduna on January twelve and thirteen.

Nzeogwu:

Yes, I am aware of that one.

Ademoyega:

And it's also been confirmed that the Commonwealth Conference that is soon to start in Lagos is also to end on the twelfth. And that most of the delegates will leave Lagos almost immediately.

Nzeogwu:

Are you sure?

Ademoyega:

Yes!

Nzeogwu:

Good! (nods his head.) If that is the case, let us fix the D-day for Saturday, January fifteen. Do you think that is okay?

Ademoyega:

Yes, it's okay!

Nzeogwu:

But if there happens to be any opportunity before the fixed day we shall strike?

Ademoyega:

It's okay. (pauses.) I've not told you.

Nzeogwu:

What?

Ademoyega:

That the Battle Group Course in the south is still on.

Nzeogwu:

Yes! Those student officers could be useful to the revolution.

Ademoyega:

I'd thought the same way.

Nzeogwu:

Have you made any move to gather the troop for our use?

Ademoyega:

Yes! (*pauses.*) I've even succeeded in meeting twenty-student officer on the course.

Nzeogwu:

Very good.

Ademoyega:

They are all captains. I succeeded in indoctrinating and orientating them towards the revolutionary thought-concept.

Nzeogwu:

Interesting. (pauses.) Are they revolutionaries?

Ademoyega:

Yes! Because I also had the opportunity to hold personal interview with all of them but that was when I took the whole group on an official reconnaissance of all the strategic installations in Lagos. (*Light fades. And from the background echoes of matching soldiers are heard. Light returns on stage, Major Ademoyega leads a group of officers onto the stage.*) Stop! (*They stop.*) This place is another strategic point. In a war situation the enemies could either come through this direction (*points*) or through this way (*pauses.*) Have you seen now that this place is strategic in the planning of this city. (*Pauses.*) If you're asked to man this point, this is how to do it. Two Officers would be walking around the point to indicate that soldiers have taken over the point, while the other officers will settle at the sides of the point for quick reaction during emergency (pauses.) You. (*points.*) You and you, demonstrate what I have just said (The two officers position themselves and start walking round the place as he instructs them. Major Ademoyega signals others to position themselves and they did) Very good! (*He claps.*) Very good! (*pauses*) Soon you will be required to carry out this duty and I'm sure you will do it well.

Officers:

We will!!

Ademoyega:

When the time comes I'll send for you. I know, you'll do it the way I've taught you.

Officers:

We will sir! (*Light gradually fades as they march out of stage. Light comes on stage again and we see Major Ademoyega and Major Nzeogwu still discussing.*)

Nzeogwu:

Did they agree to be part of the revolution?

Ademoyega:

No-o, I wasn't plain in my discussion with them. But one thing is known and that is if the revolution takes place before the course ends many of them will be willing to carry out any duty allotted to them with their back. (*Silence. Nzeogwu's phone rings and he picks it.*)

Nzeogwu:

Gbulie, it is you? (*Gbulie's voice is heard from the background*).

Gbulie:

Yes! (*pauses*) Nzeogwu it seems the Sardauna is up to something again.

Nzeogwu:

The Politicians are always at one mischief or the other, what is he up to this time?

Gbulie:

I overheard that he is also celebrating Christmas. I can't imagine a Muslim Chief celebrating Christmas.

Nzeogwu:

Really?

Gbulie:

You have not heard the latest. There is a top security meeting to be held in Kaduna.

Nzeogwu:

I am hearing it for the first time.

Gbulie:

I gathered that even Brigadier Ademulogun is joining forces with them.

Nzeogwu:

I thought he is in loggerheads with Brigadier Zak Maimalari?

Gbulie:

He has since mended his fences with Brigadier Zak Maimalari and has thrown in his lot with the almighty Sardauna.

Nzeogwu:

Really?

Gbulie:

His wife, I also gathered, is going to Mecca on pilgrimage.

Nzeogwu:

I suppose the couple are Christians.

Gbulie:

These are the information just reaching me, bye.

Nzeogwu:

Okay! (drops the phone receiver) That was Captain Ben Gbulie. He said there is a secret meeting to be held in Kaduna.

Ademoyega:

The meeting must be connected with how to wallop the West.

Nzeogwu:

How do I get a lady with whom I will go to the Sardauna's castle?

Ademoyega:

There's a lady I know in town; she will be willing to follow us.

Nzeogwu:

What are we waiting for then? Why not we start going now.

Ademoyega:

Okay, let's go! (*They walk out of the platform.*)

(Snooze)

II

Enter Major Ademoyega, pacing the stage. Enter Major Ifeajuna.

Ademoyega:

(*surprised.*) Major Ifeajuna, how'd you know I'm here?

Ifeajuna:

(*clears his throat*) I asked some people at the officers' mess and they said you've gone to the beach.

Ademoyega:

Well, don't bother to say it because I've already known what you came to say.

Ifeajuna:

You suspect too much. Okay, what do you feel I have come to tell you?

Ademoyega:

That Major Chude-Sokei has finally left for India, is it not?

Ifeajuna:

What? (pauses) Has he?

Ademoyega:

So you've not heard. He left this morning.

Ifeajuna:

Who told you?

Ademoyega:

He sent me a signal that he was leaving.

Ifeajuna:

When?

Ademoyega:

This morning, of course. (There is a long silence.) Since that's not the news, what then is the news you brought?

Ifeajuna:

You are to take a flight to Kaduna because it seems all the important personalities are in Lagos. Discuss it with Major Nzeogwu, let see whether we can strike with this opportunity. (*He puts his hand into his pocket, brings out a flight ticket and hands it over to Major Ademoyega.*)

Ademoyega:

Are you sure they're all around?

Ifeajuna:

Yes, it seems they gathered in relations to the worsening political situation in Ibadan.

Ademoyega:

Yes, what's the latest news about the riot that's going on in Ibadan? Has the Balewa government said anything about it?

Ifeajuna:

No news! The government is still pretending to be ignorant of the whole situation.

Ademoyega:

What's wrong with that government? They're making this country unsafe for Nigerians. (*pauses.*) Well, just for a little while all these will stop to happen and life will be as safe as it ought to be.

Ifeajuna:

Lest I forget, is it true that the Battle Group Course has ended?

Ademoyega:

Yes! We lost those officers who would have been of great benefit to our revolution.

Ifeajuna:

Were you able to reach Lieutenant-Colonel Fajuyi, the commander in charge of the course?

Ademoyega:

No! After the Battle Group Course ended, I was told he left for the mess immediately. I rushed down to meet him there only to be told that he merely stayed for a while after which he left for Ekiti, his home town, for holiday.

Ifeajuna:

That is to say we have lost him also.

Ademoyega:

That's exactly what it means and he would have been of a great help to our revolution. (*There is silence*)

Ifeajuna:

Are you aware of the two squads that have just arrived?

Ademoyega:

Yes! The Field Battery of Artillery and The Squadron of the Reconnaissance Corp, which are to be permanently stationed in Abeokuta. (*Major Ifeajuna nods his head, taps Major Ademoyega and they start strolling down the beach.*)

Ifeajuna:

Do you know the commanders of the two squads?

Ademoyega:

Yes! While The Field Battery of Artillery is commanded by Captain Nwobosi… (*Major Ifeajuna stops*)

Ifeajuna:

Did you say Captain Nwobosi?

Ademoyega:

Yes?

Ifeajuna:

Okay.

Ademoyega:

The Reconnaissance Squadron is command by Major Obienu. And don't worry yourself I'm still on the move to make them part of the revolution.

Ifeajuna:

(taps him and they start strolling down.) Have you met with any one of them?

Ademoyega:

Yes! I have even booked appointment with them and we're to meet today.

Ifeajuna:

Good! *(stops.)* I must leave you now.

Ademoyega:

(stops also.) Okay! *(Major Ifeajuna walks out of stage. Enter Chief H.O. Davies with a young lady. They walk up to a seat beside the Army Chalet and get themselves seated. He addresses Chief H.O. Davies, as he stands in front of him.)* Please sir. Chief H.O. Davies?

Chief Davies:

Yes! And can I help you?

Ademoyega:

Oh! I'm Major Adewale Ademoyega.

Chief Davies:

You are welcome. *(shakes hands with him.)*

Ademoyega:

Chief, it's a privilege meeting one of the politicians I adore in this country, a politician who has been in the national struggle since 1941. *(pauses.)* But sir, if I may ask, why is it that despite the fact that we have good politicians like you as ministers under the Balewa government, the government is still ineffective and inefficient?

Chief Davies:

Look Major Adewale, if you say that Balewa's government is not effective and efficient you are right. But if you say that I can do anything about it, it's untrue, because I'm merely a Federal Minister and should not be expected to pilot all the affairs of the government.

Ademoyega:

Okay, but as a Federal Minister I know you're supposed to know the plans of the Federal Government.

Chief Davies:

Yes!

Ademoyega:

What's the government's plan toward solving the problem that's raging in Ibadan and even here in Lagos?

Lady:

Please, excuse me. (*stands up and walks out*)

Chief Davies:

Listen Major Adewale, the truth to all these is that the Federal government has no solution to the political crisis.

Ademoyega:

How do you mean sir? But in his last public statement Balewa said that everything was under control (*The lady returns.*)

Chief Davies:

That is just a political statement! I wouldn't tell you lies; the Federal Government has no solution for the crisis. What we are all waiting for is to see what will happen next.

Ademoyega:

(*waves his head in bitterness.*) And what do you think might happen next?

Chief Davies:

Nobody knows exactly what that would be, but surely something is bound to happen.

Ademoyega:

Okay sir, thank you for everything. (*stands up.*)

Chief Davies:

Thank you! (*They shake hands and Ademoyega walks out of platform.*)

(Snooze)

III

Major Chukwuka's house. Enter Captain Anuforo, Major Ademoyega and Captain Udeaja.

Ademoyega:

(*to Captain Anuforo*) Are you sure nobody saw us when we came in.

Anuforo:

Nobody! (*pauses.*) But let me be sure. (*walks towards the door, opens it, looks out, comes back inside and locks the door again.*) Nobody. (*They walk up to the parlour and sit down on the available seats.*)

Ademoyega:

Captain Udeaja, the reason why Captain Anuforo and I arranged to meet you here today is to let you know the political situation of this country.

Udeaja:

(*laughs.*) Major Ademoyega but everybody knows that. I mean we all know that the political situation of this country is getting worse everyday.

Ademoyega:

But have you heard the latest? (*pauses.*) That the government of Bakwa is planning to bring the Army fully to operate in the West for the purpose of eliminating the elites of the region especially the intellectuals who they assume are behind the revolt of the people against Chief Akintola government.

Anuforo:

(*Surprised. Weaves his head*) I have not heard this myself.

Udeaja:

This is serious.

Ademoyega:

It has been said that Bakwa's government has no solution for the problem raging in Ibadan and their only way of solving the problem is through this military action.

Udeaja:

That is too bad.

Ademoyega:

I know you understand that if they are to strike, their aim will be to wipe out all oppositions in the West and if the operation yields success in the west they would face the East.

Udeaja:

I believe so too.

Ademoyega:

So it's because of this that we've called you here.

Udeaja:

Yes, I'm listening or is that all?

Ademoyega:

There's a move by a section of the army to change the cause of things in this country and we want you to be part of the group.

Udeaja:

(*looks into Major Ademoyega's face and then at Captain Anuforo's*) Very good, I'm willing.

Ademoyega:

Good! (*puts his hand into his trouser pocket, brings out a map and places it on the nearby table.*) Every other duty has been taken up by other willing soldiers. The duty that you're supposed to take up is the release of Chief Awolowo. (*pauses and stares into his face.*) Come closer so as to see the map clearly. (*Captain Udeaja comes close.*) You're to fly in a special jet, provided for the purpose to Calabar on the morning of that D-day to effect his release after which you're required to bring him back on the same jet. The jet will be made available at this location (*points to the map and stares into his face. Captain Udeaja quickly nods his head.*) This is the location where the jet will land. (*points to another part of the Map.*)

Udeaja:

Will it be a private jet or…?

Ademoyega:

No! The information on ground is that a jet of the Nigerian Air Force will be made available that morning by one Major of the Air Force.

Udeaja:

Okay! Good plan. (*They shake hands.*) Let me go and prepare myself for the task.

Ademoyega:

Okay! (*Captain Udeaja stands up and Major Ademoyega folds the map and puts it into his pocket again while Captain Udeaja walks out of platform.*)

Anuforo:

Have you been able to replace Major Chukwuka-Sokei?

Ademoyega:

Yes. We've been able to get a young officer who's now to take over the operation of Enugu.

Anufaro:

What is the officer's name?

Ademoyega:

His name is Lieutenant Ogechi, and as you know, his duty is to arrest the premier of the East, Okpara and the premier of the mid-west, Osadebay and their right hand men.

Anufaro:

Which unit does he belong?

Ademoyega:

The First Battalion, the one that's based in Enugu.

Anufaro:

Was he able to move troops from his unit?

Ademoyega:

Well, he was only able to move a platoon of thirty men.

Anufaro:

Well, he has tried his best. (pauses.) But there is still going to be problem that day because he would need a cover up order from the commander of his unit. How…?

Ademoyega:

Forget it? Everything is under control You know the First Battalion based in Enugu is under the operational command of the Second Brigade based in Apapa of which Major Ifeajuna is the Brigade Major.

Anuforo:

Very good, that is to say Major Ifeajuna will give him a cover up order. This is the correct military procedure. Little wonder he complied.

Ademoyega:

We're now waiting for the D-day since the last opportunity didn't click.

Anuforo:

What really happened that day?

Ademoyega:

On that day most of the important personalities suddenly came to Lagos then Major Ifeajuna gave me the flight ticket to Kaduna. Instead of flying to Kaduna immediately, I sent a signal that I was coming and almost immediately Major Nzeogwu replied it saying that there was no need. According to him, the Sardauna and other Northern leaders are still in Mecca in relation to the Umra Hadji.

Anuforo:

(*shocked.*) eh! (*jumps up.*)

Ademoyega:

What's it?

Anuforo:

Wale, we are doomed. Look, there is nothing stopping Captain Udeaja from revealing the whole plan to Lieutenant-Colonel Arthur Unegbu with whom he is known to be quite close.

Ademoyega:

(*shocked.*) And of course, Lieutenant-Colonel Unegbu will immediately give the whole plan to Brigadier Maimalari who in turn would relate everything to Bakwa (*stands up.*) And we would be doomed without having struck any blow. (*pauses.*) Let's go after him. (*They run out of platform.*)

(snooze)

IV

Enter Captain Udeaja, walking towards the road. Enter Captain Anuforo and Major Ademoyega, panting.

Anuforo:

Thank God! (*points.*) Look at him going? He is just going to see him.

Ademoyega:

Where're you going? (*to Captain Udeaja.*)

Udeaja:

I'm going to see Lieutenant-Colonel Unegbu (*walks pass them.*)

Ademoyega:

Stop! (*He stops.*)

Anuforo:

We will like to talk with you.

Udeaja:

(*turns to them.*) I'm listening.

Ademoyega:

Captain Udeaja, we're not saying that you should call off your relationship with Lieutenant-Colonel Unegbu but the danger of revealing the plan to him will fear.

Udeaja:

Lieutenant – Colonel Unegbu is not like that; he's not a talkative person.

Anuforo:

It's better he is not told at all so that there will be no risk to face.

Ademoyega:

Do you understand what Captain Anuforo said?

Udeaja:

(*stares into Major Ademoyega's eyes and then into Captain Anuforo's face.*) Okay, I'll not go to see him until after I've carried out my duty.

Ademoyega:

Good! (*They shake hands again and Captain Udeaja walks out of platform.*) God saved us! (*gasps.*)

Anuforo:

We would have been doomed.

Ademoyega:

Let's get out of this place. (*walking away.*)

Anuforo:

Wake wait! (*pauses.*) Don't you think if we don't backdate the D-day, the Bakwa government would succeed with their operation for the west before we strike? (*pauses.*) And you know that will make nonsense of our revolution.

Ademoyega:

The information reaching us has it that they'll not strike until Sarduana comes back from Mecca. But while he's away they will finalize all their plans on how the operation would be effectively carried out. And as you know, the Sarduana will come back on the twelfth or thirteenth and while they relax trying to plan on how to strike the west, we'll take them unaware on the fifteenth.

Anuforo:

Interesting!

Ademoyega:

As you can see they're already at work. The government is now doing a lot of reshuffle in the Army. For instance Lieutenant-Colonel Gowon has taken over the Ikeja Battalion, Major-General Ironsi has been ordered to proceed on leave from mid-January and to be relieved by Brigadier Maimalari, over the head of Brigadier Ademulegun. Lieutenant-Colonel Njoku is to temporarily command the Second Brigade Headquarters at Apapa after which he would be posted to another Brigade. And the Inspector-General of the Police Force, Edet, has also be asked to proceed on leave while the officer closest to him is retired so as to give way for the officer under him, Alhaji kam Salem. So Alhaji kam Salem is now to be the new Inspector-General.

Anuforo:

(*laughs.*) Ah! The stage is now set for them to wallop the UPGA rioters of the West. (*pauses.*) But Wale, are there ready troops for the Abeokuta operation?

Ademoyega:

Yes, Captain Nwobosi of the Field Battery of Artillery and Major Obienu of the Reconnaissance Squadron are now for us. They promised to turn out troops that day, for the Abeokuta Operation.

Anuforo:

Interesting! Everything is set. Let me go and get myself prepared. *(They shake hands and walk out of platform.)*

(Snooze)

(ACT THREE)

I

Enter a group of officers in platoon, often. Enter Major Ifeajuna, Captain Anuforo, Major Okafor, Major Chukwuka, and Major Ademoyega.

Ifeajuna:

(*clears his throat and speaks to Major Ademoyega*) Why are Major Obienu and Captain Udeaja not here yet?

Ademoyega:

It's not zero, two, zero, zero hours yet. Let's wait. I'm sure they will soon arrive. (*lowers his voice*) Which task are you allotting to Major Okafor?

Ifeajuna:

The arrest of the G.O.C.

Ademoyega:

That's a more sensitive task. Give it to another officer or even me. Major Okafor is not competent enough to handle that task.

Ifeajuna:

Don't worry; he is in the right position to do it. I know he will (*pauses*) Meanwhile, let's send officers for rifles. (*Major Ifeajuna beckons on Major Chukwuka and whispers into his ear. Major Chukwuka leaves the stage, followed by two subalterns.*) Are you sure Major Obienu and Captain Udeaja will come? (*glances at his wristwatch*) It's time!

Ademoyega:

Then start!

Ifeajuna:

(*clears his throat. Faces the soldiers*) The current political development threatens the foundation of this country and therefore calls for urgent intervention. And as a matter of fact, there is a nationwide operation by a section of the Army to return the lost peace and unity to the country. And now that the moment of action has come, it is essential for all of you to whom this responsibility rests upon to fight for your country. (*The crowd of officers cheer. Some want to leave and were persuaded to stay. Enter Major Chukwuka and the two subalterns with bags of rifles. The rifles are shared among officers.*) Captain Anuforo and one subaltern should go and arrest Colonel K. Mohammed and Lieutenant-Colonel Unegbu. (*Captain Anuforo signals the subaltern beside him to follow him and they walk out of platform.*) Major Okafor, one Captain and a subaltern should arrest Major-General Ironsi and Brigadier Maimalari. (*Major Okafor, a captain and a subaltern walk out of platform.*) Major Chukwuka and one subaltern are to arrest Lieutenant-Colonel Pam. (*Major Chukwuka and a subaltern walk out of stage.*) Major Ademoyega, a Captain and two subalterns are to occupy and control all strategic locations including the control room at lion building, the P and T and external telecommunication operation room. And are also to make the early morning broadcast over the NBC. (*As Major Ademoyega prepares to leave with his group, Major Ifeajuna calls him back.*) Wake, remember also to contact Captain Nwobosi and Lieutenant Ogechi. Order them to go ahead with the operation of Ibadan and Enugu respectively.

Ademoyega:

Okay! (*gathers his group and leaves the stage.*)

Ifeajuna:

1, Major Ifeajuna, and the rest of you are to arrest the Prime Minister, Sir Abubakar, the Federal Minister for finance, Chief Okotie Eboh and to make sure troops from different commands are available for use. (*pauses*) So, every one of you should get into his combat suit and bear his arm for the operation. (*Soldiers rush out of platform and Major Ifeajuna follows them.*)

(Snooze)

II

Enter Captain Anuforo's group with Lieutenant-Colonel Unegbu.

Subaltern:

(*pushes him*) Move! (*Lieutenant-Colonel Unegbu staggers forwards. They stop at Colonel K. Mohammed's mess.*)

Anuforo:

(*turns to the Subaltern.*) This is Colonel K. Mohammed's mess. While I go to arrest him, stay here with Lieutenant-Colonel Unegbu. He must not escape!

Subaltern:

Yes sir! (*Captain Anuforo walks into the mess. Subaltern turns his rifle to Lieutenant-Colonel Unegbu.*) Face the wall! (*He refuses. Subaltern hits him with the rifle.*) Face the wall! (*He refuses. Captain Anuforo emerges with Colonel K. Mohammed.*)

Anuforo:

Okay! Colonel! Mohammed, face the wall! (*He faces the wall and Major Anuforo turns to the Subaltern.*) Tie his hands. (*Subaltern ties his hand.*) Lieutenant-Colonel Unegbu should also face the wall! (*He refuses. Subaltern hits him again.*)

Subaltern:

He is too stubborn.

Anuforo:

There is no time for this. (*shoots at him severally. Lieutenant-Colonel Unegbu falls to his face. Major Anuforo turns to Colonel K. Mohammed.*) Move! (Colonel K. Mohammed complies and they walk out of stage.)

****

Prime Minister's residence. A police orderly is sitting and reading a newspaper and the guards are busy pacing up and down the stage. Enter Major Ifeajuna's group.

Ifeajuna:

Don't move! (*The newspaper falls from the police orderly while the guards freeze.*) Lie down! (*They comply.*)

Sir Abubakar:

(*from inside*) Who is there? Will somebody answer me? I say who is there? (*Major Ifeajuna and two Subalterns walk into the lounge and later come out with him.*)

Ifeajuna:

(*to Subalterns*) The two of you should go and arrest the Minister of Finance. (*The two Subalterns walk out.*)

Sir Abubakar:

Please don't kill me. I will give you anything you want. Please don't kill me! (*They push him as they walk. The Subalterns return with Chief Okotie-Eboh, arrested.*)

Okotie-Eboh:

(*begging.*) Please don't kill me. Please don't kill me. (*Enter Brigadier Maimalari with a police sees major Ifeajuna and runs towards him.*)

Maimalari:

Major Ifeajuna, there is… (*They shoot him and he falls.*)

Sir Abubakar:

Kai! I am finished. Please don't kill me o! (*They walk out of stage.*)

****

The receptionist is busy writing. Enter Major Ifeajuna and his group.

Receptionist:

Welcome to Ikoyi Hotel. How do I help you?

Ifeajuna:

I want you to give me the master key which could open all the doors in the hotel.

Receptionist:

(*frightfully*) There is no key like that under my possession.

Ifeajuna:

Okay, take us to the room where Lt. Col. Largema is. (*The Receptionist is visibly shaking.*) Move! (*She comes out from the counter.*) Young lady, I want you to comply with whatever we ask you to do, if you do, you will not be shot.

Receptionist:

Okay sir! (*leads them to the room down stage*)

Ifeajuna:

Knock! (*The receptionist stares into his face and quickly knocks*)

Largema:

(*from inside*) Who is there?

Ifeajuna:

Speak!

Receptionist:

Sir, you are wanted at the telephone.

Largema:

Okay, I will be there.

Ifeajuna:

(*to the Receptionist*) Go away. (*She runs out. Lt. Col. Largema comes out dressed in pajamas and he is shot.*)

(Snooze)

III

Enter Major Ademoyega's group and Captain Anuforo's group with arrested Colonel K. Mohammed.

Ademoyega:

I know Lieutenant - Colonel Unegbu has refused arrest.

Anuforo:

(*cuts in*) And has been shot.

Ademoyega:

Good Job! (*Enter Major Chukwuka's group with the arrested Lieutenant-Colonel Pam.*) Here comes Major Chukwuka and his group.

Anuforo:

Thank God, they were successful (*Enter Major Ifeajuna's group with the arrested Prime Minister and the Federal Minister of Finance.*)

Sir Abubakar:

Please, don't kill me. I'll give you pounds. (*The subalterns beat him for mentioning money.*)

Ifeajuna:

(*clears his throat*) Is Major Okafor's group back?

Ademoyega:

No!

Ifeajuna:

I'm not sure everything is all right with him because while we were returning we saw Brigadier Maimalari escaping from the attempt of his group to arrest him. We tried to arrest him ourselves but he resisted and in the scuffle he was shot. (*pauses.*) Let's look for him. (*Enter Major Okafor all alone, holding his head in his two hands.*)

Here, he comes.

Ademoyega:

What happened to you? What have you achieved?

Okafor:

(*slowly*) I've just lost my command. (*They all shouted.*)

Ademoyega:

What's all this about?

Okafor:

I spoke to my RSM just now and he nearly shot me. He said the GOC had been to the barracks. I quickly rushed to that place but couldn't meet him there.

Ademoyega:

What? (*pauses.*) Did he escape?

Okafor:

I went to his house to arrest him but I found out that he was not there. He had not yet returned from the party.

Ademoyega:

Which party? (*gasps.*) Everybody had left the party since nine, last night.

Okafor:

No, it was another party. He had gone to another party after Brigadier Maimalari's party and now he had gone to my barrack and had commanded the troops not to take any order from me and none of them will obey me now. In fact they were ready to shoot me.

Ifeajuna:

We are doomed! (*pauses.*) Major Okafor, do you know that troop is our hope for this Lagos operation?

Ademoyega:

If we can no longer use Major Okafor's federal guards, which other troops can we use? (*pauses.*) Which troop can we rely upon? (*There is silence.*) But Major Okafor, why's it that your own group did not achieve anything? (*Major Okafor is silent.*)

Ifeajuna:

There is a problem now. We must get Ironsi before he gathers troops against us. But first of all, (*turns.*) you, (*points.*) you and you, take these arrested officers to the bush and shoot them! (*Soldiers take Colonel K. Mohammed, Lieutenant-Colonel Pam and others out of stage. Several gunshots are heard from the background and the soldiers return on stage.*)

(Snooze)

IV

Enter Major Nzeogwu with a bleeding leg and a Doctor with a first-aid box. The Doctor treats Nzeogwu. Enter soldiers.

Subaltern I:

What happened to him?

Subaltern II:

He was wounded during our attack on the premier's lodge.

Subaltern I:

Did the premier resist arrest?

Subaltern II:

Yes! (*pauses.*) Even when he noticed that his mighty gate had been blown off with five rounds of the eighty-four mini meters Carl Gustav anti-tank recoilless rifle, which even set the walls of the gate on fire.

Subaltern I:

Did he escape?

Subaltern II:

No! He… (*The stage suddenly becomes dim, eight beams a little below the stage. Enter Major Nzeogwu's group. At the corner of the lowered stage is a room. The soldiers position themselves with their guns pointing menacingly at the door.*)

Nzeogwu:

Everybody come out with your hands up! (*Sardauna and his wives come out, crying, screaming and sobbing.*) Where is the Sardauna? (*The wives shout in protest and rush to surround the Sardauna. The Sardauna moves away from the women, removes the white veil on his face and is shot. Light move down stage and we are returned to the former scene.*)

Subaltern I:

That serves the Sardauna right! But how did Major Nzeogwu sustain the injury?

Subaltern II:

He sustained the injury when the gate exploded. (*Enter Major Onwuatuegwu's group with the arrested Sir K. Ibrahim.*) Here comes Major Onwuatuegwu and his prisoner.

Nzeogwu:

(*walks towards them and orders the handcuffs to be removed. The handcuffs are removed and Nzeogwu shakes him.*) You are a good man, (*pauses*) It is not against people like you we have staged this coup. It is because of all those corrupt politicians who for the past five years have been holding this country to ransom without rhyme or reason. (*turns to Onwuatuegwu.*) Get me that document that is prepared for the politicians. (*Major Onwuatuegwu leaves and returns with the document.*) Sir Ibrahim, you are going to sign this document but let me read it to your hearing: (*reads*)

Whereas the government of the Northern Region of the Federal Republic of Nigeria has lost the confidence of the governed, and whereas the said Northern Regional government is no longer able to guarantee the safety of human lives as well as the rule of law in its area of jurisdiction, I Sir Kashim Ibrahim, on whose shoulders the gubernatorial powers of the said Northern Regional government have rested since independence, having been myself the accredited custodian of the constitution in this same region, do hereby, on this day, Saturday, the 15th of January, 1966, relinquish to the Nigerian Armed Forces all those powers, statutory or otherwise hitherto exercised by my government. (*hands him the document and Sir Ibrahim signs it. Nzeogwu turns to Major Onwuatuegwu*) Major Onwuatuegwu, please let him go.

Onwuatuegwu:

(*hands Sir K. Ibrahim over to the Subalterns.*) Take him out and please don't touch him because he has been behaving himself. (*They lead Sir K. Ibrahim out of platform.*)

Nzeogwu:

What of Brigadier Ademulegun? Did he resist arrest?

Onwuatuegwu:

Yes! (*Light fades again and comes back on stage. Enter Major Onwuatuegwu's group. Enter Brigadier Ademulegun in a short trouser, going to urinate.*)

Onwuatuegwu:

That must be Brigadier Ademulegun.

Subaltern I:

What is he doing there? Is he aware of this operation?

Subaltern II:

Perhaps, he is taking fresh air.

Onwuatuegwu:

(*to Brigadier Ademulegun.*) Don't move! (*He sees them and is shocked.*) Hands up! (*He complies.*) You (*points.*) tie his hands. (*Brigadier*

Ademulegun suddenly wants to escape.) He has escaped! (*They shoot him and he falls and dies. Light fades and we see Major Nzeogwu and Major Onwuatuegwu on stage again.*) While I was returning I saw Captain Gbulie's group, they are really doing a nice job. They are in perfect control of all the strategic points in the City. (*Enter Captain Ude and his group.*)

Nzeogwu:

Captain Ude, what happened?

Ude:

Colonel Shodeinde resisted arrest and has been shot.

Nzeogwu:

Good job! (Captain Ude walks inside.)

Onwuatuegwu:

(smiles.) We are now in control of the North.

Nzeogwu:

Not yet! We still have a problem.

Onwuatuegwu:

What is the problem?

Nzeogwu:

The problem is how to contact other unit commanders in the city and make them support the revolution. If they support us, that is only when we can claim total victory of the North.

Onwuatuegwu:

If that is the case, let's send Major Keshi, the revolution staff officer to those commanders.

Nzeogwu:

Will Major Keshi do a good job?

Onwuatuegwu:

Yes! He knows how to reach them. He has worked under many commands here in the North. (Enter Captain Ude.)

Nzeogwu:

Thank God Captain Ude is here (*to Captain Ude*) Tell Major Keshi that he is wanted here. (*Captain Ude walks out of stage.*) I know that even if Major Keshi claims he can reach all of them, it is not normal to order him into carrying out all commands. At least I can reach Lieutenant-Colonel Bassey of the Nigerian Army Depot, Zaria by sending him a letter.

Onwuatuegwu:

Better!

Nzeogwu:

You think so too? (*beckons on a nearby subaltern and he marches forward.*) Get me a pen and some papers. (*The subaltern walks out of the stage.*) I know Major Hassan U. Katsina of the Nigerian Reconnaissance Corps and Lieutenant-Colonel Ojukwu of the fifth Battalion Kano will not be moved by a mere letter. They would need to be confronted.

Onwuatuegwu:

Why not try them with letters first.

Nzeogwu:

You may be right; to prevent unnecessary risk I suppose.

Onwuatuegwu:

Yes! (*The Subaltern comes in with a pen and some papers. He collects them from him and drafts some letters. Enter Captain Ude and Major Keshi.*)

Nzeogwu:

Good, you are here now. Captain Ude, I want you to deliver this letter to Lieutenant-Colonel Bassey. (*Major Nzeogwu gives him the letter and turns to Major Keshi.*) While you are to deliver this one to Major Madiebo and Lieutenant-Colonel Ojukwu. Tell them that we are in full control of the North and that they should be friends of the revolution or face the wrath of being its enemies. (*gives him the letter and they leave the stage.*) Send a signal to our men in the south, tell them that we are still waiting for their broadcast, while I meet with Major Hassan U. Katsina to gain his loyalty.

Onwuatuegwu:

Okay! (*walks out of stage. Enter Captain Gbulie.*)

Nzeogwu:

(*stops as he sees him.*) Thank God you are here. Stay here and monitor the activities of the revolution.

Gbulie:

Okay! (*Major Nzeogwu leaves the stage.*)

(Snooze)

(ACT FOUR)

I

Enter soldiers, positing themselves beside the door of Nigeria Broadcasting Corporation. Enter Captain Anuforo and Major Ademoyega with their troops.

Ademoyega:

My God, Ironsi's troops have taken over the NBC. What should we do? Should we shoot our way in to make the broadcast?

Anuforo:

You know they are more than we are. Had it been that Major Ifeajuna, Major Okafor and Major Chukwuka and their groups are still with us it would have been easier.

Ademoyega:

Major Ifeajuna, Major Chukwuka and Major Okafor have made a mess of this whole struggle. Where's their whereabouts? (*pauses*) Or have they been arrested?

Anuforo:

(*bittered.*) The worst of it all is that I'm sure Major-General Ironsi roused the Second Battalion against us. The same troops Major Obienu promised to make available for our use.

Ademoyega:

Anuforo, let's still look for Ironsi. We must get him before he makes a broadcast.

Anuforo:

I'm not sure he would show himself because I know he is aware that we are after him. That must be the reason he is not steady in his hideouts. For instance, we went to Ikoyi to get him, we were told he had left for the NBC, we are now here and he is not here again.

Ademoyega:

Let's send one of our Officers to those men to see if we can penetrate the NBC.

Anuforo:

Okay, let's try it. (*An officer is sent to penetrate into the NBC. He walks up to the soldiers waiting in front of the door. They stop him. He tells them in mime that he wants to go in and they signal him to go back. He refuses and tries to struggle himself in. They cock their rifles and point them towards him and Major Ademoyega intervenes.*)

Ademoyega:

Don't shoot! Don't shoot! (*They force the soldier to face the wall and press their rifles against his head*) Why do you want to shoot him?

Soldier I:

Major-General Ironsi ordered us not to allow any body into the NBC.

Soldier II:

He said we should arrest any unfriendly force.

Ademoyega:

And who're the unfriendly forces?

Soldier I:

He never told us. So anybody who tries to go into this place by force automatically becomes it.

Ademoyega:

Leave him alone! I was the one who sent him. (*They hit him and release him.*) Where can we see Major-General Ironsi now?

Soldier:

We don't know!

Ademoyega:

Okay, thank you. (*leaves with the officer and they return to Captain Anuforo and the troops.*) Those officers are working under serious order from Ironsi. They would not allow anybody into the NBC unless over their dead bodies.

Anuforo:

What do we do now?

Ademoyega:

I think the best thing to do is to send some of our officers afield in search of him.

Anufuro:

Okay, let's try it out!

Ademoyega:

(*turns to his troop.*) You, (*points*) you and you, go in search of Major-General Ironsi. If you see him come back and tell us or if possible kill him. (*They leave the stage.*)

Anufuro:

What do we do next?

Ademoyega:

Let's return to the Federal officers' Mess. He might have returned to the mess. (*They were about to leave when all of a sudden there comes a broadcast from the radio.*)

Broadcast:

(*from the background.*) There has been an attempt by a dissident section of the Nigerian Army this morning. The Prime Minister, Sir Abubakar Tafawa Balewa and the Federal Minister of Finance, Chief Festus Okotie-Eboh, were apprehended and taken to an unknown destination. A government statement in Lagos today says that the General Officer Commanding the Army, Major-General Aguyi-Ironsi and the vast majority of the Army remained loyal to the Federal Government and are taking all effective measures to bring the situation under control. The statement adds that the Federal Government is satisfied that the situation will soon return to normal and that the ill-advised mutiny would be brought to an end and that law and order in the two disturbed areas of the country will soon be restored. (*As soon as the squadron subaltern who has been with them hears it, he feels horrified. He quickly summons the troop he came with and signals them to follow him. Major Ademoyega and Captain Anuforo try to stop him. He quickly brings out his pistol against them. They stop while he leaves the stage with the troop.*)

Anuforo:

Wale, it is now clear that we have lost Lagos. (*pauses.*) And you know we can't go to Enugu to gather troops because of this recent radio announcement.

Ademoyega:

Let's leave this place before we fall victim of Ironsi's troops. (*pauses.*) Let's board train to Kaduna

Anuforo:

Are you sure the revolution has not also failed in the North.

Ademoyega:

No, it can't fail there. (*pauses.*) Let's go. Maybe they may need our help. (*They walk out of Platform.*)

(Snooze)

II

Enter Major Nzeogwu, Major Onwuatuegwu, Captain Ude, Captain Gbulie, Major Keshi and Soldiers.

Nzeogwu:

We are now in control of the North, since we have got the support of other unit commanders. (*pauses.*) Major Onwuatuegwu, were you able to reach our men in the south?

Onwuatuegwu:

No! I sent signals to them but no reply came. In fact things are not okay with them there. (*Enter a Captain.*)

Captain:

There is an announcement against the revolution but the Prime Minister and the Federal Minister of Finance are said to be missing.

Nzeogwu:

That is to say we have lost the south and must make the announcement that we are in control of the North.

Gbulie:

That is just what we ought to do now.

Nzeogwu:

We have run short of finance. Captain Ude, I want you to meet Lieutenant-Colonel Ojukwu to collect the money he promised to make available for the deployment of troops. Major Keshi, go to the town and gather the people and the press. Let's make our own broadcast. (*Captain Ude and Major Keshi walk out of stage.*) Major Onwuatuegwu and Captain Gbulie go and monitor the activities of revolution. (*They walk out of stage followed by soldiers. After a little while enter Major Keshi and the people together with the press. The staff of the Nigerian Broadcasting Corporation of about three people mount their camera after which Major Nzeogwu makes his broadcast.*)

Nzeogwu:

In the name of the supreme council of the revolution of Nigerian Armed Forces, I declare Martial law over the Northern Province of Nigeria. (*pauses.*) The constitution is suspended and the regional government and elected assemblies are hereby dissolved. The aim of the revolutionary council is to establish a strong, united and prosperous nation, free from corruption and internal strife. You are hereby warned that looting, arson, homosexuality, rape, embezzlement, bribery or corruption, obstruction of the revolution, sabotage, subversion, false alarms and assistance to foreign invaders are all offences punishable by death sentence. (*pauses.*) Like good soldiers we are not promising anything miraculous or spectacular. But what we do promise every law-abiding citizen is freedom from fear and all forms of oppression, freedom from inefficiency and freedom to live and strive in every field of human endeavour. We promise that you will no more be ashamed to say that you are Nigerians. (*pauses.*) My dear countrymen, this is the end of my speech. I wish you all good luck and hope you will co-operate to the fullest in the job, which we have set for ourselves. Thank you very much and good-bye for now. (*Major Nzeogwu stops and walks out while the soldiers lead the people out of stage.*)

(Snooze)

III

Major-General Ironsi is seen seated on a cushion. Enter Lieutenant-Colonel Gowon and Major Madiebo.

Ironsi:

Sit down. (*They sit.*) I've been told that Major Nzeogwu and his men are planning to carry their fight to the south. How true is it, Major Madiebo?

Madiebo:

Very true sir. They have succeeded in summoning the civil servants in the North and have also succeeded in making them loyal to their revolutionary principle.

Gowon:

Has he also gained the loyalty of all the commands in the North?

Madiebo:

I think most of the units and commands are now loyal to him.

Ironsi:

What can we do now?

Madiebo:

Something can be done. I suggest we stage a palace coup.

Ironsi:

Okay, Major Madiebo go and befriend him. Make sure you discourage him from carrying the fight to the south.

Madiebo:

How would I do it?

Ironsi:

Just let him see reasons and now go!

Madiebo:

I pray I'm able to make him give up the fight. (*leaves the stage.*)

Gowon:

What if he refuses?

Ironsi:

If he refuses? (*pauses.*) That automatically means that he is crazy over power and not what he claims. (*pauses.*) Meanwhile I want you to contact his very good friend, Lieutenant-Colonel Nwawo. Lieutenant-Colonel Nwawo would make him understand that he is supposed to hand over power to a superior officer.

Gowon:

Okay!

Ironsi:

(*pauses.*) Let's see if a palace coup would work?

Gowon:

Okay!

Ironsi:

Go and co-ordinate it. (*Lieutenant-Colonel Gowon stands up and leaves the platform.*)

(Snooze)

(ACT FIVE)

I

Enter captain and subalterns armed.

Captain:

Ah! You (*to a Subaltern*) make sure all soldiers coming into this place are those with whom we conquered this town. Do you hear?

Subaltern I:

Yes sir! (*Enter two other Captains armed.*)

New Captain:

No one of you should move! (*The soldiers want to open fire on them and all of a sudden the two captains shoot and the other captain falls.*)

(Snooze)

****

Enter Major Onwuatuegwu, Captain Gbulie and other soldiers.

Onwuatuegwu:

We must fight to the south to release our men who have been arrested there.

Gbulie:

The fight is very important for this struggle. It is the only way forward for this revolution. (*Enter a Subaltern. He rushes towards Major Onwuatuegwu.*)

Subaltern:

There is news that Lieutenant-Colonel Ojukwu has arrested Captain Ude who was sent to collect some money for the troops' use.

Onwuatuegwu:

I've always known Lieutenant-Colonel Ojukwu to be crafty. After pretending to be in support of the revolution he turned around and arrested a soldier who was sent to him. (*Enter Major Nzeogwu and more soldiers.*)

Nzeogwu:

Our next line of action is the fight towards the South. (*Enter a soldier.*)

Soldiers:

One of our units has been taken over by soldiers loyal to Major-General Ironsi and all our revolutionary soldiers there have been either killed or brought to their knees.

Nzeogwu:

(*enraged.*) Okay! (*faces the soldiers.*) I am dividing this troop into three crack task forces. The first task force is to move North, taking Zaria and Kano, to consolidate the control of those areas and make themselves available for the southern operation. The second task force is to advance southwest through Jebba to Ibadan. It is to take Ibadan and prepare the ground for launching into Lagos. While the third task force is to advance southeast to Enugu through Makurdi. It is to take Enugu and launch southwest to take Benin and to hold two regions firmly for the revolution. (*Enter Major Madiebo. Major Nzeogwu sees him and pauses.*) Please excuse me. *(to the soldiers.)*

Madiebo:

Are you preparing to carry on with the battle?

Nzeogwu:

Yes! We are about starting the fight.

Madiebo:

(*claps.*) That's Good! (*smiles and glances at the ready soldiers.*) Major Nzeogwu, look I'm your friend and wouldn't tell you lies. This revolutionary battle is very unnecessary.

Nzeogwu:

How do you mean.

Madiebo:

I was with Ironsi yesterday on your behalf. I told him to surrender because you are already in control of the North.

Nzeogwu:

And what did he say?

Madiebo:

He said he admires your courage and the cause in which you have fought, but you know, his concern is the procedure of leadership in the Army. It is only on that ground that he said you should surrender the Northern Province to him so that the dream with which you fought could be realized. And he promised to make you a member of the Military Ruling Council in Lagos.

Nzeogwu:

Major-General Ironsi should go to hell with his deceit. Our course is for a better Nigeria and not a lust for power.

Madiebo:

That is even the reason why you should cancel your plan of fighting towards South and surrender to Ironsi who is in the right position to carry out your revolutionary plans.

Nzeogwu:

How do you mean? (pauses.) Look at these soldiers! (*points at the prepared revolutionary soldiers.*) They are waiting for me; they are prepared to fight for this country.

Madiebo:

I haven't said you shouldn't carry on with your battle. What I am only saying is that fighting down south wouldn't yield result. You won't be allowed to do it, you're a junior officer.

Nzeogwu:

Major Madiebo, please no more of this. Just go for now. I shall send for you later.

Madiebo:

Okay, let me go! (*Leaves the stage. Major Nzeogwu returns to the soldiers.*)

Nzeogwu:

There is news that Ironsi wants us to settle matters like gentlemen. Let's wait until we hear what he has to say. (*The soldiers dismissed Major Onwuatuegwu, Captain Gbulie and Major Keshi come to him.*) Major Madiebo said Ironsi is ready to settle with us like gentlemen.

Onwuatuegwu:

Do you trust him?

Nzeogwu:

Nobody talks about trust here. (pauses.) His reason and why we should try to negotiate with Ironsi is cogent.

Keshi:

What did he say?

Nzeogwu:

He said the battle is unnecessary because even after the battle we would still have to allow an officer who is up to the rank of a General to govern the country.

Keshi:

What if we refuse?

Nzeogwu:

We will lose the supports of officers above the rank of Major.

Gbulie:

It is true. The battle is unnecessary. (*Enter Lieutenant-Colonel Nwawo. Major Nzeogwu sees him.*) My goodness! Who am I seeing? Lieutenant Colonel Nwawo. So you are back from London.

Nwawo:

Yes! (*pauses.*) I was told what you are doing, so I said I must come and see you and tell you to carry on with your hard work. It is wonderful and not also easy.

Nzeogwu:

It is not time for praises yet. We are in dilemma now …

Nwawo:

Dilemma over Ironsi's threats? Forget it!

Nzeogwu:

How do you mean?

Nwawo:

I've been with him on your behalf and we discussed for a very long time.

Nzeogwu:

What did he say?

Nwawo:

His problem is not the revolution but that you are a junior officer. (*pauses.*) I told him I'll see you. After which he said I should ask you to give him your conditions.

Nzeogwu:

Can I speak to him myself?

Nwawo:

I will make arrangement for that. (*pauses.*) Let me go and arrange your meeting. (*leaves the stage.*)

Nzeogwu:

(*commands.*) Soldiers, guide the revolutionary territory we expect Ironsi.

Onwuatuegwu:

You said Ironsi is coming to this place?

Nzeogwu:

Yes: (*pauses.*) I want him to affirm that Major Madiebo and Lieutenant-Colonel Nwawo said.

Onwuatuegwu:

Okay! (*pauses.*) Prepare your rifles! (The Soldiers prepare to shoot.)

Nzeogwu:

If he comes and disagrees with our conditions we shoot him and bring down his soldiers. (*Enter Major-General Ironsi, Lieutenant-Colonel Nwawo and Soldiers. The Revolutionary soldiers point their rifles towards Major-General Ironsi and his soldiers.*)

Ironsi:

Major Nzeogwu, tell your men to put down their rifles. (*Major Nzeogwu signals the soldiers and they put down their rifles.*) I want you to surrender the Northern Province to me so that I can help make the dream with which you fight come through.

Nzeogwu:

What made you think I can be deceived into handing the North over to you so easily?

Nwawo:

Major Nzeogwu, let us settle this thing like gentlemen. Look, I'm your friend and will not be party to anything that will bring you down.

Nzeogwu:

Okay! (*pauses.*) I will not surrender the North to him, except he accepts my conditions.

Ironsi: Yes, that is why I am here.

Nzeogwu:

My conditions are as follow: First, you must not hand over power to the civilians whom we fought to remove. Secondly, all those who took part in the coup must not be punished. Thirdly, we must be given a chance to be part of the ruling council so that we can help shape the country in accordance with how we have dreamt it.

Ironsi:

(*pauses.*) Accepted. (*Major General Ironsi and his soldiers leave the stage, while Lieutenant Colonel Nwawo stays behind.*)

Nwawo:

That's Okay! (*pauses.*) You see, I told you he would accept your conditions. (*Enter Major Ademoyega and Captain Anuforo.*)

Nzeogwu:

(*Happily.*) My God! So you are alive? (*Major Onwuatuegwu, Captain Gbulie and Major Keshi rush forward and embrace them.*)

Onwuatuegwu:

Thank God you are alive. What of Major Ifeajuna, Major Chukwuka and Major Okafor?

Ademoyega:

We don't know their whereabouts.

Gbulie:

How do you means?

Ademoyega:

Captain Anuforo and I went to check our road blocks and to ask the men we mounted there if they knew Ironsi's whereabouts only to come back to realize that Major Ifeajuna and others with whom we agreed to go to Ibadan for more troops that would match Ironsi's had gone.

Nzeogwu:

What really happened; how did you lose Lagos?

Anuforo:

Major Okafor missed Ironsi.

Onwuatuegwu:

What was his excuse?

Ademoyega:

That's a long story. Let's not go into it. (*pauses*) I've heard so much about your victory here.

Nzeogwu:

It wasn't easy at all. We thought you have all been killed or arrested and planned fighting to the south...

Anuforo:

Great! Let's begin. (*Major Ademoyega cheers.*)

Nzeogwu:

But... (*They become quiet again.*)

Ademoyega:

But what?

Nzeogwu:

I have been advised not to carry on with the fight.

Anuforo:

Why?

Nzeogwu:

Because it will make us more ambitious than revolutionary.

Ademoyega:

How?

Nzeogwu:

Because Major-General Ironsi has vowed to accept any condition I put forward to him.

Anuforo:

I don't understand this.

Nzeogwu:

Captain Anuforo, Major Ademoyega, look I believe that our dream is for a better Nigeria, so carrying the battle to the south makes no sense of it since Ironsi has accepted our conditions and those corrupt politicians will be no more.

Ademoyega:

Have you given him the conditions?

Nzeogwu:

Yes.

Anuforo:

What are the conditions you gave him?

Nzeogwu:

That he must not hand over power to civilians. Secondly that all those who took part in the coup must not be punished. Thirdly, that we should be given the chance to be part of the ruling council.

Ademoyega:

Very good!

Anuforo:

Are you sure we can trust him?

Nzeogwu:

That is another thing. (*pauses*) I'll contact other unit commanders who are in support of the revolution to advise me on this issue. (*Enter a soldier.*)

Soldier:

Captain Ude has been released. I saw him coming. (*Enter Captain Ude. They embrace him one after the other.*)

Ude:

I was released on the ground that Ironsi negotiated with you.

Nzeogwu:

That is to say Ironsi is sincere. (*turns to Lieutenant-Colonel Nwawo*) You said it.

Nwawo:

I won't deceive you.

Nzeogwu:

(*turns to his colleagues.*) This is Lieutenant-Colonel Nwawo, a good friend of mine. He just came from London.

All:

You are welcome.

Nzeogwu:

(*to Captain Anuforo and Major Ademoyega.*) I know you need rest now. Let's go inside. (*They walk out of stage.*)

(Snooze)

II

The Brigade headquarters, Kaduna. Enter people, taking their positions a little below the platform. Enter armed soldiers, positioning themselves at the corner of the platform. Enter Major Hassan and Major Nzeogwu. The National Anthem is played. Soldiers stand at attention and then parade the stage, saluting Major Nzeogwu who stands like a statue at a corner of the platform. After the parade, Major Hassan addresses the people.

Hassan:

(*clears his throat*) Today marks the beginning of a new era in the history of this nation. (*pauses, looks at Major Nzeogwu and then to the people.*) Major Nzeogwu is one man in whom I have seen the trait of so much selflessness. He is a man whom all soldiers should try to emulate. (*pauses*) For me, I promise to stand by those principles and purposes for which he fought. Thank you. (*applause from the background. He comes down from the rostrum, walks towards Major Nzeogwu and embraces him. They shake hands and Major Nzeogwu hands over power to him. Another applause. Major Nzeogwu salutes him. The National Anthem is played again. Enter Lieutenant-Colonel Nwawo, Major Ademoyega, Captain Anuforo; Major Onwuatuegwu, Captain Ude, Major Keshi and Captain Gbulie.*)

Nzeogwu:

Wake, I am going to Lagos now with Lieutenant-Colonel Nwawo to take up the appointment as a member of the ruling council.

Ademoyega:

(*happily*) Go! All's well

Anuforo:

We know you will not forget us.

Nwawo:

Let's go!

Nzeogwu:

Okay, Good-bye! (*They all leave the stage.*)

****

Enter Major Anuforo and Major Ademoyega, terrified.

Anuforo:

Wake, Major Nzeogwu has landed into the hands of Major-General Ironsi's gunmen.

Ademoyega:

I don't understand. What of all the promises?

Anuforo:

Major Madiebo and Lieutenant-Colonel Nwawo have only succeeded in deceiving him.

Ademoyega:

Lieutenant-Colonel Nwawo, his very good friend?

Anuforo:

We are finished! How do we get them? How can we get the rest of us?

Ademoyega:

Major Onwuatuegwu and Captain Ude have resumed with N.M.T.C. Kaduna. We can always reach them.

Anuforo:

Let's go and tell them so that we can plan the next action to take. (*They run out of platform.*)

****

Kirikiri Maximum prison. Enter Major Okafor, Major Chukwuka, Major Onwuatuegwu, Captain Gbulie, Major Keshi, Major Nzeogwu, Captain Anuforo, Captain Ude, Lieutenant-Colonel Banjo, Captain Nwobosi and Major Ademoyega. The sound of a fastened gate is heard from the background.

Onwuatuegwu:

Is this not Lieutenant-Colonel Banjo? *(turns to Lieutenant-Colonel Banjo.)* What are you doing here?

Banjo:

They said I'm one of you because I said our revolution is justified, and that you should be released.

Nwobosi:

Our problem in this country is that we don't want to tell ourselves the truth.

Ademoyega:

Major Ifeajuna is the cause of this whole thing. I told him on time that he shouldn't give that sensitive task to Major Okafor but he did.

Nzeogwu:

Wale, forget it! We have all made our mistakes.

Anuforo:

Who knows where Major Ifeajuna is now.

Okafor:

He has gone out of the country. His poet friend, Christopher Okigbo drove him in his car to the border between Nigeria and Dahomey.

Anuforo:

Where did he say he was going?

Okafor:

To Ghana. (*The sound of an opened gate is heard. Enter Major Ifeajuna led by a Subaltern.*) Oh, here he comes. (The Subaltern leaves the stage and the sound of a fastened gate is heard again.)

Ademoyega:

Ifeajuna what happened? (*Major Ifeajuna remains silent.*) Is it true that you ran to Ghana when the revolutionary child whom you helped to conceive was about to be delivered?

Ifeajuna:

(*clears his throat*) What do you expect me to do? Major General- Ironsi was after us.

Ademoyega:

(*enraged*) Major General Ironsi shouldn't be the excuse now, knowing that you're the soul of our Lagos operation!

Ifeajuna:

I don't think…

Ademoyega:

(*slaps him.*) You don't think what? (*They start fighting. Major Onwuatuegwu and Captain Ude stand up, trying to separate them. There is a sharp blackout.*)

THE END

[1] I featured Ademoyega more than the other plotters not because I intend to make him the hero of the coup but because the greater part of the plot was carved out from his book *Why We Struck*. Other details were gotten from other books, which includes: *Madiebo's The Nigerian Revolution and the Biafra War*, *Gbulie's Nigerian's Five Majors*, *Mainasara's The Five Major: Why They Struck*, *Ojukwu's Because I am Involved*, *J.Isawa Elaigwu's Gowon*, *Zdenek Cervenka's A History of the Nigerian War 1967*, *Nelson Ottal's Rebels*, *Okeleke Nzeogwu's Major C K Nzeogwu: Fighting the illusive Nigerian Enemy From Childhood to Death*.

Mmap Fiction and Drama Series

If you have enjoyed *The Last Revolution* consider these other fine books in Mmap Fiction and Drama Series from *Mwanaka Media and Publishing*:

The Water Cycle by Andrew Nyongesa
A Conversation…, A Contact by Tendai Rinos Mwanaka
A Dark Energy by Tendai Rinos Mwanaka
Keys in the River: New and Collected Stories by Tendai Rinos Mwanaka
How The Twins Grew Up/Makurire Akaita Mapatya by Milutin Djurickovic and Tendai Rinos Mwanaka
White Man Walking by John Eppel
The Big Noise and Other Noises by Christopher Kudyahakudadirwe
Tiny Human Protection Agency by Megan Landman
Ashes by Ken Weene and Umar O. Abdul
Notes From A Modern Chimurenga: Collected Struggle Stories by Tendai Rinos Mwanaka
Another Chance by Chinweike Ofodile
Pano Chalo/Frawn of the Great by Stephen Mpashi, translated by Austin Kaluba
Kumafulatsi by Wonder Guchu
The Policeman Also Dies and Other Plays by Solomon A. Awuzie
Fragmented Lives by Imali J Abala
In the Beyond by Talent Madhuku
Zororo Risina Zororo by Oscar Gwiriri
Sword of Vengeance by Olatubosun David
Finding A Way Home by Tendai Mwanaka
Your Epistle by Solomon A Awuzie
The Restless Run and Ruin of the Roaches and Rats by McLayode
The Reign of Terror by Ntando Gerald
Ibala Lyabwina Nama by Austin Kaluba

Daddy, Please Don't Kill Mama by Natisha Parsons
Pilate's Angels by Goodenough Mashego
Blue threads and other stories by Matthew Kunashe Chikono
The Sylvia Plath Effect by Abigail George
The Twins by Shakemore Dirani
I, Robert's Robot and other stories by Marvel Chukwudi Pephel
Conversation With My Mother by Wonder Guchu
Stranger In Her Own Skin by William Mpina
Zimbolicious 10th Anniversary, Fictions by Tendai Rinos Mwanaka
The Kule Tokwe Diaries by Hosea Tokwe
Burying Ghosts by Samuel Chuma

Soon to be released

https://facebook.com/MwanakaMediaAndPublishing/

www.ingramcontent.com/pod-product-compliance
Lightning Source LLC
Chambersburg PA
CBHW071008160426
43193CB00012B/1963